Fantastic Creatures

First published in 1999 by Macdonald
Young Books, an imprint of Wayland
Publishers Limited, 61 Western Road, Hove,
East Sussex, BN3 1JD

Paperback edition first published in 2000
by Macdonald Young Books

Commissioning editor: Hazel Songhurst
Project editors: Hazel Songhurst and Lisa
Edwards
Design: Chris Leishman
Illustration: Douglas Gray
Front cover illustration: Colin Sullivan

Picture acknowledgements:
Bridgeman Art Library: 27(c) (National
Gallery, London; Bruce Coleman: 19(c)
(Gunter Ziesler); Mary Evans Picture
Library: 7, 9(tl), 19(tr), 24(cb); Fortean
Picture Library: 9(br) (René Dahinden),
10(tr) (Cliff Crook), 16(ct), 17(tr), 25(tl);
Images Picture Library: 15(cb) (Charles
Walker Collection); Rex Features: 13(cb)
(Dave Lewis); Science Photo Library: 22(br)
(Makota Iwfuji/Eurelics), 27 (Mehau Kulyk);
Topham Picturepoint: 11 (Associated
Press), 16(tl), 20(tl).

A CIP catalogue record for this book is
available from the British Library

ISBN 0 7500 2766 5

Ivor Baddiel was a primary school
teacher before becoming a full-time
writer and broadcaster.

Tracey Blezard is an English-language
teacher and a writer specializing in
teenage fiction.

MYSTERIOUS WORLD

Fantastic Creatures

Investigations into the unexplained

Ivor Baddiel & Tracey Blezard

MACDONALD YOUNG BOOKS

Contents

About this book

Is Bigfoot just a giant gorilla or a creature that is half-man, half-ape? Do terrifying monsters lurk deep in our oceans? Could fairies be real beings? Is the Loch Ness Monster actually a prehistoric dinosaur? And is it possible that bloodthirsty vampires and werewolves actually exist?

Throughout the ages, people have caught glimpses of weird and wonderful creatures, many of which remain as mysterious today as they

were thousands of years ago. But while some people dismiss them as the stuff of myths and legends, others firmly believe that these magical creatures actually existed and that perhaps, in some remote corners of the world, they still do. Today, when we look for evidence of their existence, we turn to science.

But long before there were scientific explanations, people relied on mythology to explain the world around them. A myth is neither scientific fact, nor fiction. Religious historian, Mircea Eliade, wrote: 'Myths tell only of that which really happened.' So although they could be based on fact, the truth may have then become blurred and exaggerated over the centuries.

In this book, we provide the information you need to try and unravel the facts from the fantasy, the real monster from the myth. For each mystery, study the evidence, consider the latest popular theories, read what the scientists have said and then decide for yourself.

Monster? Myth? Extinct creature or undiscovered species? Maybe you will be the one to finally uncover the truth...

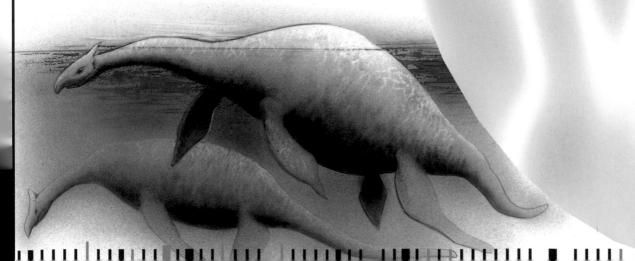

Wild Men

It goes by different names, depending on where in the world it is found: the Abominable Snowman or Yeti in the Himalayas, Bigfoot or Sasquatch in North America, Yeren in China, Nguoi Rung in Vietnam and Orang-Pendek in Sumatra. With so many reported sightings of these human-like apes, should we admit that something strange is roaming the world's forests and mountains?

? THE MYSTERY

Could these shaggy, human-like 'wild men' be our distant relatives, ferocious monsters or simply giant monkeys?

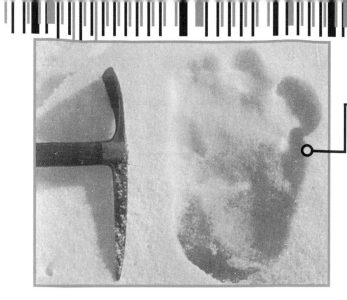

In 1951, 30 kilometres west of Mount Everest, mountaineer Eric Shipton photographed massive footprints in the snow. They have never been identified. In 1980, footprints in the mountains of central China were thought to belong to a creature very similar to early man. Casts taken of giant human-like footprints found in a US forest in 1982 were examined by scientists who concluded they were from an unidentified creature.

On 20 October 1967 in California, hunter Roger Patterson filmed an ape-like creature walking off into the forest. The film shows a creature almost 2 metres tall and, judging from the footprints it left, weighing considerably more than a fully grown gorilla. In 1997, naturalist Chris Packham used the same camera to re-enact the footage. He was surprised at how close Patterson would have needed to be to get the film and that the ape had shown no interest in him.

THE EVIDENCE

The oldest recorded Bigfoot sighting dates back to 986 AD, when Viking explorer Leif Erikson landed in America and wrote of 'hairy monsters with great black eyes'.

In the 18th century Swedish scientist Carolus Linnaeus invented the system for classifying animals. He firmly believed that these strange creatures were neither human nor monkey but something in between.

In 1925 Russian soldiers shot dead what may have been a Neanderthal 'man-ape', thought to have died out 40,000 years ago. The hairy, human-like creature had a flat nose, prominent jaw and sloping forehead.

The 1950s and 60s saw a series of Yeti hunts throughout the Himalayas. British explorer, Sir Edmund Hillary, led one such quest and brought back the scalp and skin of what he believed to be an Abominable Snowman.

A British mountaineer on Mount Annapurna believed that the thief who stole chocolate from his tent was a Yeti!

THE EVIDENCE

In **1969** a 'man-ape' encased in a block of ice was discovered in North America. It had an ape-like toe but the padded feet of a human being. Mystery still shrouds the 'Minnesota Ice-Man' as it was withdrawn from public investigation before scientists could decide on its origins.

1,089 giant footprints made by some creature seemingly able to clear high fences in a single stride, were tracked in Canada.

Scientists exploring the dense Indonesian forests hope to glimpse the giant orange-haired ape thought to live there, which they believe to be distantly related to human beings.

THE THEORIES

Missing Link These creatures are indeed linked to human evolution. In isolated forests and mountains, they have been able to survive undisturbed for centuries.

Apes What is being sighted is an orang utan, or the langur monkey, which often stands upright.

Mistaken Identity A 'Yeti skin' was found to be the skin of a blue bear which had strayed from its native territory and was unknown to observers. Such cases of mistaken identity can explain all sightings of this kind.

Melting Snow Footprints found in snow appear bigger than they really are due to the snow melting, refreezing and so distorting their shape and size.

Giant monkeys The Yeti is the sole survivor of a huge ape *Gigantopithecus* that lived throughout Asia until about 300,000 years ago.

Superstition People of the Himalayas have believed in the Yeti for centuries but sceptics claim it is a superstition passed down through generations.

Hoaxes What we are really seeing is a person in a gorilla suit playing a practical joke.

WHAT SCIENCE SAYS

Scientists remain unconvinced about the existence of wild men. They point out that despite the latest technology, such as time-lapse photography and infra-red beams to pick up the giant's movements, the only 'evidence' remains the distant sightings of eye witnesses and some footprints. They insist that by now we would have uncovered some more convincing evidence of this half-man, half-ape such as a captured specimen or, at the very least, bones and carcasses.

What Do You Think?

Could Bigfoot be so clever as to continually outwit hunters?

How could a distant human ancestor have survived almost in secret until today?

If scientists were to capture a live Yeti, what do you think they should do with it?

If the creature doesn't want us to know about its existence, shouldn't we leave it alone?

Could there be other animals around the world that we know nothing about?

Giants

Compare the average adult male height of 1.7 metres with that of the world's tallest ever man, American Robert Wadlow, who grew to 2.7 metres. Could there once have been many more people who reached these gigantic proportions?

 ## THE MYSTERY

Are giants found only in legends or did a race of them once inhabit the Earth?

 ## THE EVIDENCE

In Greek mythology terrifying, people-eating, one-eyed giants struck fear into the heart of anyone who had the misfortune to meet them. They were called Cyclopes ('round eye') because of the huge, single eye in the middle of their foreheads.

In the 15th century, a huge skeleton was unearthed in Sicily. The skull had a single hole in it and was thought to be the remains of a Cyclops.

THE THEORIES

Elephant fossils So-called Cyclopes skulls were in fact those of elephants. The 'eye socket' was the hole for the trunk.

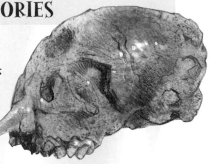

Extinct race Just as giant dinosaurs became extinct, there was once a race of giant people who died out.

Myths and legends For centuries, stories of giants have been popular. Belief in them has been fuelled by the occasional discovery of an over-sized skeleton.

In the Bible story, the giant Goliath is said to have been more than 3 metres tall.

Human skeletons, over 2.5 metres long, were unearthed on Lundy, off south-west England, suggesting that giants once inhabited the island.

Until his death in 1998, Pakistani Haji Mohammad Alam Channa was the world's tallest man at 2.3 metres.

Many Dinka tribespeople of southern Sudan are well over 2 metres tall.

 ## WHAT SCIENCE SAYS

Medical giants do exist. The condition known as gigantism causes people's bodies to grow much bigger and faster than normal, especially the bones of the face, feet and hands. True giants may not be the fierce, blood-thirsty monsters of stories, but they are real.

What Do You Think?

What advantages are there to being a giant?

Why might a race of giants have died out?

Could one huge eye be better than two small eyes?

If giants have never existed, why were they invented?

Mysteries of the Deep

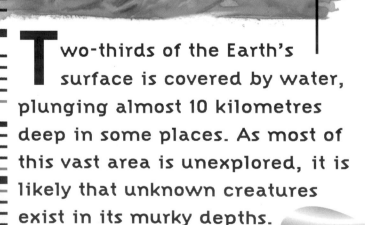

THE MYSTERY

From singing mermaids to ship-munching monsters: are these the ramblings of delirious sailors or the accounts of terrified eye-witnesses?

THE EVIDENCE

In 1848, the captain of the British ship *Daedalus* described a sighting in the South Atlantic of 'a sea serpent' 18 metres long that reared its snake-like head over a metre out of the water. It was brown with a yellowish throat and a mane.

Two-thirds of the Earth's surface is covered by water, plunging almost 10 kilometres deep in some places. As most of this vast area is unexplored, it is likely that unknown creatures exist in its murky depths.

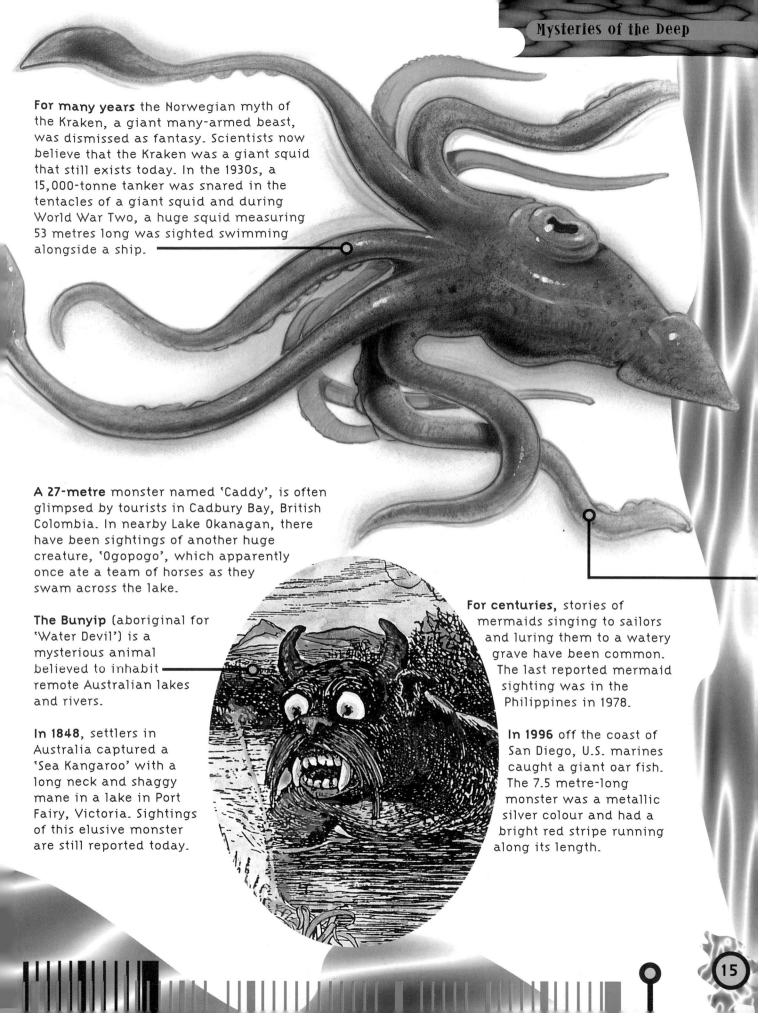

For many years the Norwegian myth of the Kraken, a giant many-armed beast, was dismissed as fantasy. Scientists now believe that the Kraken was a giant squid that still exists today. In the 1930s, a 15,000-tonne tanker was snared in the tentacles of a giant squid and during World War Two, a huge squid measuring 53 metres long was sighted swimming alongside a ship.

A 27-metre monster named 'Caddy', is often glimpsed by tourists in Cadbury Bay, British Colombia. In nearby Lake Okanagan, there have been sightings of another huge creature, 'Ogopogo', which apparently once ate a team of horses as they swam across the lake.

The Bunyip (aboriginal for 'Water Devil') is a mysterious animal believed to inhabit remote Australian lakes and rivers.

In 1848, settlers in Australia captured a 'Sea Kangaroo' with a long neck and shaggy mane in a lake in Port Fairy, Victoria. Sightings of this elusive monster are still reported today.

For centuries, stories of mermaids singing to sailors and luring them to a watery grave have been common. The last reported mermaid sighting was in the Philippines in 1978.

In 1996 off the coast of San Diego, U.S. marines caught a giant oar fish. The 7.5 metre-long monster was a metallic silver colour and had a bright red stripe running along its length.

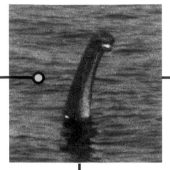

Perhaps the most famous creature of all is the Loch Ness monster, said to dwell in the black depths of Loch Ness, Scotland. In 1987, *Operation Deepscan'* s sonar equipment picked up movements of an unidentified giant 73 metres below the lake's surface. Mysterious clicking noises have also been recorded.

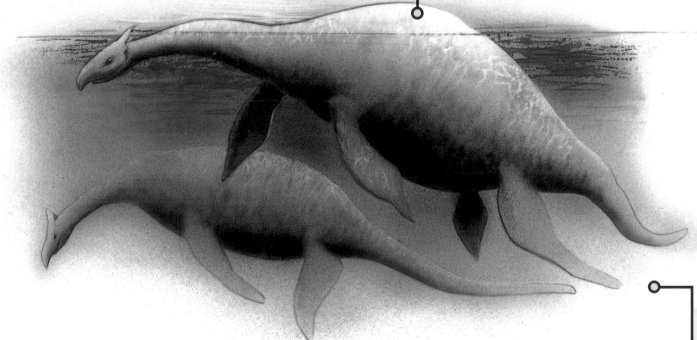

Over a thousand eye-witnesses have reported glimpsing the monster but there have also been numerous hoaxes. A famous photograph taken in 1934 fooled scientists until 1994, when the owner admitted the 'monster' was a model stuck onto a toy submarine.

The creature photographed by Dr. Robert Rines in 1975, appeared in publications worldwide. Named *Nessiteras Rhombopteryx* (Ness Wonder With Diamond Shaped Wing) by naturalist Sir Peter Scott, was it just a coincidence that Nessiteras Rhombopteryx is an anagram for 'Monster Hoax By Sir Peter S'?

 # THE THEORIES

Deep-sea fish Little-known sea creatures, such as the oar fish (which is only sighted alive about 3 times a century) could easily be mistaken for sea serpents.

Prehistoric creatures Many 'monsters' are in fact dinosaurs left from prehistoric times. This belief has been strengthened by the capture this century of live coelacanths – fish that were previously thought to have been extinct for 70 million years.

Seals Long ago, sailors mistook dugongs, manatees and seals for mermaids. The cries of these creatures can sound very human and they sit on rocks just as mermaids are often pictured.

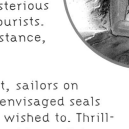

Hoaxes People fake reports of mysterious creatures for fame or to attract tourists. The area around Loch Ness, for instance, has a thriving tourist industry.

Imagination runs wild In the past, sailors on board ships for months at a time envisaged seals as beautiful women because they wished to. Thrill-seeking adventurers saw whales and large fish as savage monsters they could do battle with.

WHAT SCIENCE SAYS

As with UFOs, scientists point out that a lack of formal identification does not make an unexplained creature a mysterious monster. Previously unknown species are constantly being found. The massive megamouth shark, for example, was only discovered in 1976.

Scientists also dismiss the popular idea that lake-dwelling monsters such as 'Nessie' are plesiosaurs: air-breathing, prehistoric dinosaurs thought to be extinct 65 million years ago. This is because plesiosaurs lived in oceans not freshwater lakes. Moreover, Loch Ness has only existed since the last Ice Age. 'Nessie' and other strange monsters are more likely to be kinds of giant eel or long-necked seal, as yet unidentified.

What Do You Think?

If you encountered a sea monster, how would you get people to believe you?

How would you cope spending weeks or months alone at sea?

If you saw an unknown creature for the first time, wouldn't you call it a monster?

Would you go swimming in Loch Ness?

How would you survive if a giant squid attacked your boat and threw you into the water?

Werewolves and vampires

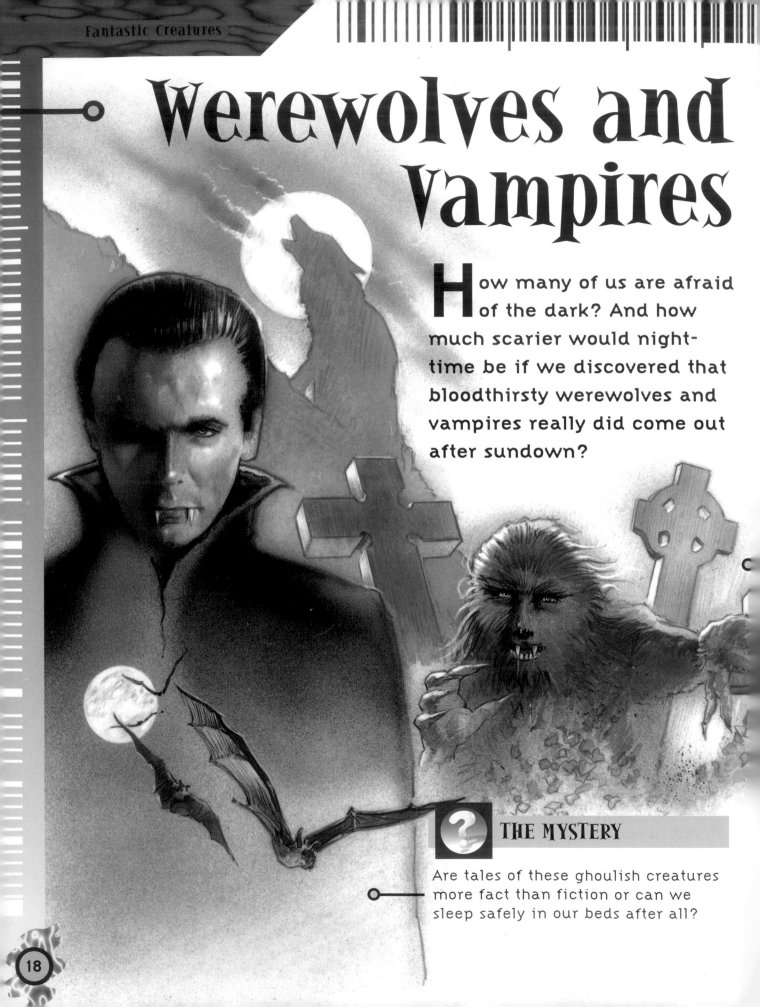

How many of us are afraid of the dark? And how much scarier would night-time be if we discovered that bloodthirsty werewolves and vampires really did come out after sundown?

? THE MYSTERY

Are tales of these ghoulish creatures more fact than fiction or can we sleep safely in our beds after all?

THE EVIDENCE

Throughout history there have been cases of abandoned children being brought up by wolves, such as the 'wolf boy' found roaming a French forest in 1797 and the 'wolf children' of Midnapore in Northern India rescued in 1920.

According to medieval legend, anyone who survived the bite of a wolf would then turn into one. This terrible curse was believed to pass from father to son. Some victims could turn into a wolf at will, while in others it was brought on by the full moon.

In the Middle Ages throughout Europe, suspected werewolves were made to stand trial. In France between 1520 and 1630, 30,000 such trials were held.

Vampire bats really exist. They inhabit Central and South America and feed on sleeping animals by puncturing their skin and painlessly sucking out the blood.

In 1987 a British man gave himself up to police believing he was a werewolf, but then turned on them, arching his fingers like claws and fighting for 4 hours before finally being sedated. The police said that the man showed 'extraordinary strength and animal-like behaviour'.

Bram Stoker's 1897 novel *Dracula*, has inspired many modern vampire tales. The story may have been based on bloodthirsty historical figures such as Erzsebet Bathory who lived in 16th-century Hungary. She murdered many people and drank their blood. Another possible source was the 15th-century Romanian prince, Vlad Dracul Tepes – a barbaric military leader.

Vampires are thought to be the dead who return to life and feed on the blood of the living. Tales of terrifying creatures rising from their graves at night to attack human beings have been found all over Europe, in Iceland, Trinidad, Borneo and Mongolia.

Stories exist where the graves of people who had 'died' some years before, were opened to reveal bodies that appeared to have only just passed away. In Eastern Europe in 1732, the grave of a suspected vampire was reportedly opened to reveal a healthy, sleeping man!

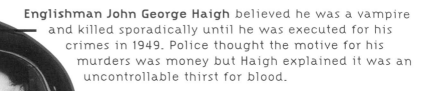

Englishman **John George Haigh** believed he was a vampire and killed sporadically until he was executed for his crimes in 1949. Police thought the motive for his murders was money but Haigh explained it was an uncontrollable thirst for blood.

In 1970, vampire expert Alan Blood took part in several vampire hunts in Highgate Cemetery, London. Witnesses claimed to have seen a gliding human-like shape and discovered damaged graves.

THE THEORIES

- **Mental Illness** The medical condition known as lycanthropy is the belief that a person can change into a wolf. Disturbed individuals may also believe they are vampires.

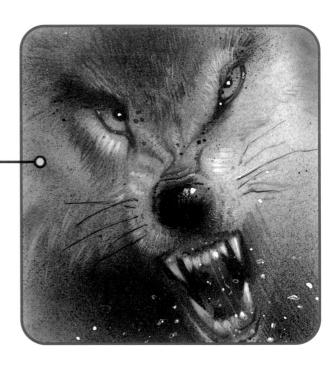

- **Rabies** The belief that a person bitten by a wolf would turn into one probably stemmed from the disease rabies carried by these animals. Anyone bitten would quickly become wild and disorientated and froth at the mouth.

- **Ancient instincts** The animal instinct is within us all and dates back to when we had to hunt for food in order to survive.

- **Homelessness** In times of great poverty, it is possible that homeless people broke into tombs, sheltering inside and hunting at night for food. Glimpsed in the dark, they may well have been mistaken for ghoulish monsters.

Porphyria This rare disease results in hair growth, mental confusion, muscle contractions that reveal the teeth and the need to hide in dark places – all typical werewolf characteristics.

Religious myth Long ago, Christians kept alive the vampire superstition to show people what would happen to their souls if they left the church.

Premature burial Sometimes people were accidentally buried alive and upon waking could have been mistaken for vampires.

 ## WHAT SCIENCE SAYS

To date, scientists remain adamant that these monsters exist only in the minds of those suffering from mental or physical disorders. The term 'haematomania' means 'a lust for blood' – this mental condition may account for the behaviour of some aggressive, bloodthirsty people.

What Do You Think?

Is your best friend a werewolf?

Why are vampires always evil?

If a true werewolf were ever captured, should it be punished?

Do you feel a little strange when there is a full moon?

Would you go to a cemetery at midnight?

Why are people afraid of the dark?

Mutant Monsters

In the story of Frankenstein, a creature was created that was half-human, half-monster. But tales of mutant animals have existed throughout history.

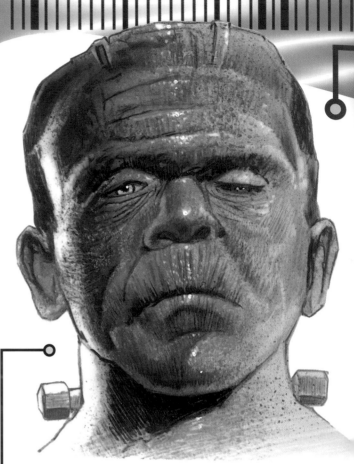

 ## THE MYSTERY

With today's advances in genetic engineering, has the Frankenstein legend finally come true?

Today peculiar breeds are a scientific fact: in the 1990s the world's first 'geep' (half-sheep, half-goat) was created by mixing together cells from different embryos. A two-headed snake has been engineered; and a mouse injected with the genes of a jellyfish, turning it luminous green.

 ## THE EVIDENCE

The Ancient Egyptian sphinx had a human head and the body of a lion. According to legend, it set a riddle for passers-by and devoured those who got it wrong. The riddle was 'What creature walks on four legs in the morning, two at noon and three at night?'*

The Ancient Greeks believed in a chimera: a fire-breathing creature with the head of a lion, the body of a goat and a serpent's tail.

*Answer: Man – crawls on all fours in the 'morning' of life; walks on two legs as an adult; and uses a stick in the 'evening' of life.

In 1991 Astrid the 'human pig' was born, so-called because the protein in her skin cells is human. Scientists now hope to breed pigs with humanized organs for transplant operations.

A New York scientist is trying to be the first to patent his method for creating half-human, half-animal mutants – to stop less-responsible scientists from doing so.

WHAT SCIENCE SAYS

Today scientists have the power to alter the genes of all kinds of plants and animals, and genetically modified foods are already available in supermarkets. The creation of mutant animals, such as the geep, is already a scientific fact but it is likely to be many years before this knowledge is put to widespread use.

THE THEORIES

Hoaxes Many of the mutants from olden days were fakes, constructed by sailors out of dry skate and ray skins.

A volcano The legend of the fire-breathing goat could have come from the Chimera volcano in Asia. Lions roamed around the top, goats around the middle and snakes and lizards at the bottom. At a distance, together with the flames from the volcano, the whole mountain looked like a giant, fire-breathing mutant.

Extinct monsters Strange creatures, now extinct, existed in ancient times.

Ancient wisdom Long ago, our ancestors knew the secrets of genetic engineering, the results of which were weird cross-bred monsters.

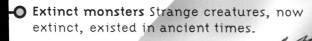

What Do You Think?

Should scientists interfere with nature?

Would you mind eating genetically altered food?

Could the mythological creatures have been early attempts at cross-breeding?

If half of your body had to be that of an animal, what animal would it be?

Little People

For hundreds of years, people believed in the 'little people', tiny nature spirits that included pixies, goblins, elves, leprechauns and sprites, along with the butterfly-winged fairies of story books.

THE MYSTERY

Could these magical little beings actually exist?

THE EVIDENCE

Good and bad fairies are part of many cultures worldwide. Celtic myth expert, Dr. W. Evans-Wentz, maintains that they exist as invisible spirits.

Cousins Frances Griffiths and Elsie Wright from Yorkshire, England, caused a storm of controversy in 1917 when they photographed themselves playing with fairies. In 1983 the cousins admitted that Elsie had made the fairies from card (left) – all except in the photograph 'The Fairy Bower' which clearly shows transparent fairy creatures and a chrysalis. To her dying day, Frances insisted that she had seen real fairies.

17th-century Welsh girl Shui Rhys, claimed she often met with the little people. One day she just disappeared without trace.

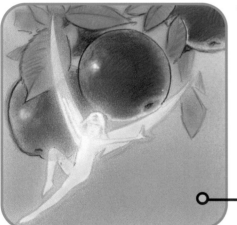

In the 1940s, servicemen on the Isle of Man found that their vehicles mysteriously cut out when they tried to cross the Fairy Bridge of Balla-g-Lonney. Locals explained that they first needed to greet the elves and fairies. When the airmen started to raise their hats to the little people the problems ceased.

At Findhorn, a remote spiritual community in Scotland, giant crops grow on poor soil thanks to the aid of nature spirits, or so the inhabitants believe.

WHAT SCIENCE SAYS

In Ireland in 1959, archaeologist A. McLean May discovered the remains of three distinct civilizations dating back to 7,000 BC. There were tunnels so small they could only have been used by midgets. He believed the occupants came to Ireland soon after the last Ice Age and could have given rise to the legends of Irish leprechauns, Scandinavian trolls and English fairies.

What Do You Think?

If a fairy granted you three wishes, what would they be?

Have you ever blamed something or someone else for something you've done?

Should we believe in what we cannot see?

Why might little people wish to stay hidden from us?

THE THEORIES

- **Pygmies** A race of miniature gnome-like people has always existed but in the past were recalled more as fairies and elves than real people.

- **Imagination** These creatures are a part of our childhood that many of us want to keep alive.

- **Spirits** Invisible forces exist in the world around us and are interpreted as 'fairies'.

- **Scapegoats** A belief in mischievous pixies is a convenient excuse when things go wrong.

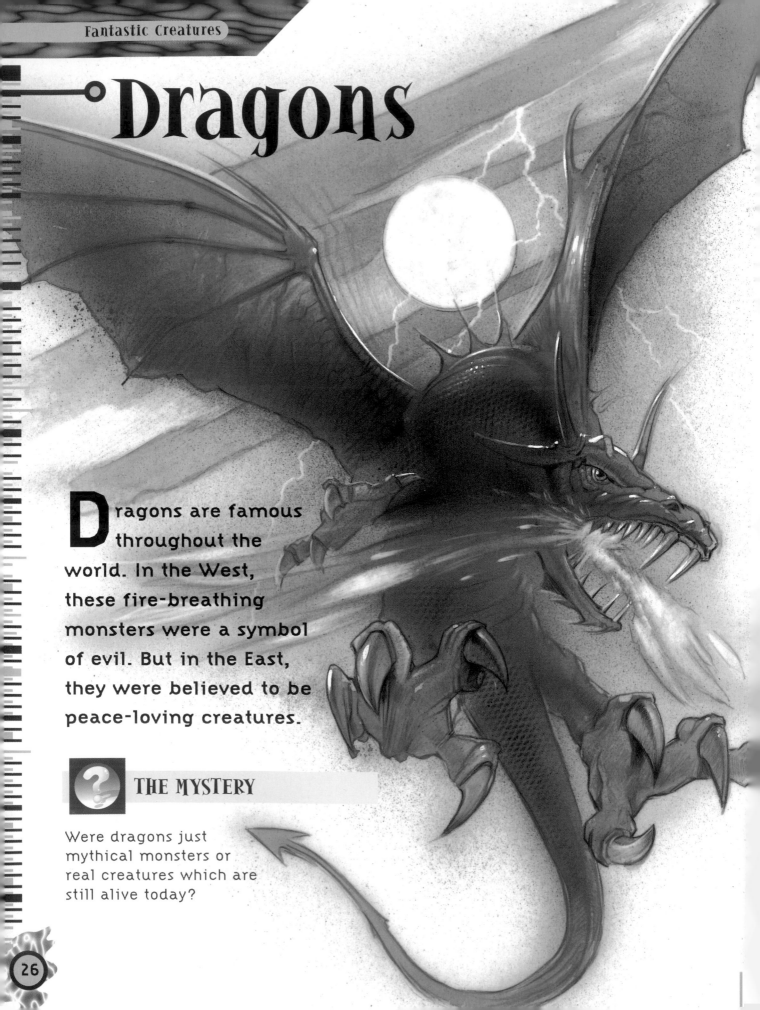

Dragons

Dragons are famous throughout the world. In the West, these fire-breathing monsters were a symbol of evil. But in the East, they were believed to be peace-loving creatures.

? THE MYSTERY

Were dragons just mythical monsters or real creatures which are still alive today?

THE EVIDENCE

In the East, dragons were believed to live in the heavens and control the weather: their breath created the clouds and the pressure of their feet brought the rain.

Dragon stories have been told in the West since the Middle Ages and were an important symbol in Christianity. To defeat a dragon meant defeating evil.

In the tale of St. George, England's patron saint, a ferocious dragon lived in the swamps of Silene, Lebanon, spreading terror with its evil, fiery breath. The desperate king tied his daughter to a stake as a sacrifice. As the thrashing beast reared up from the reeds, the brave knight St. George slayed it with a single blow from his sword.

Ancient travellers venturing into new lands came across unknown creatures such as giant snakes, lizards and crocodiles which may have inspired stories of dragon-like monsters. Explorers returning from India spoke of 'dragons' like giant serpents, which strangled their victims by coiling tightly around them.

Many dragon legends have been traced back to dinosaur fossil sites and it is quite possible that people originally believed the dinosaur bones were those of dragons.

One dragon-like creature still living is the Komodo dragon, the world's largest lizard found on Komodo Island in South-east Asia. Its flickering tongue resembles the fiery breath of legendary dragons.

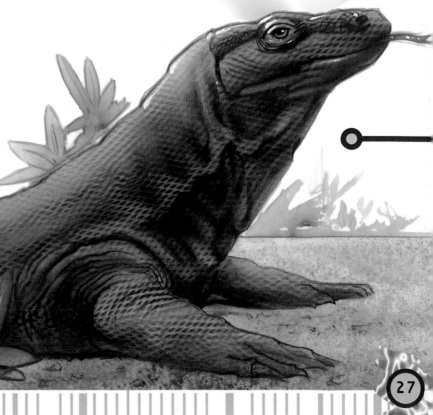

THE THEORIES

Mythology Today, science explains natural phenomena such as thunderstorms. Without scientific knowledge, people found other explanations to make sense of their world.

Ancient animals Real creatures such as mammoths, woolly rhinos and dinosaurs may have inspired stories of the legendary dragon.

Religious myth The dragon was a symbol of evil adopted by Christianity, used to scare unbelievers.

Tall tales Explorers exaggerated stories of animals they encountered. Sometimes fear caused their minds to distort the true image into a more terrifying beast.

Giant reptiles A fierce creature that lived in rivers and swamps may just have been a crocodile or lizard. The huge Indian python, or alligators that inhabit the Yangtze River in China, for example, could easily have been mistaken for monsters.

UFOs Extraterrestrials have been visiting the Earth for centuries and early sightings of spaceships were thought to be flying dragons.

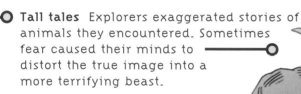

WHAT SCIENCE SAYS

Our understanding of ancient creatures comes largely from unearthing their fossilized remains. The fact that no dragon remains have been discovered suggests that they never existed. They were either real beasts that were mis-identified by early travellers, or simply the stuff of stories. However, of the estimated 30 million animal species that have existed on Earth, only a small number have so far been uncovered.

What Do You Think?

How could you describe a tiger if you really wanted to exaggerate its features?

How might dragons have produced the fire they breathed?

How do you think a dragonfly got this name?

If dragons were popular in tales long ago, what creatures are most popular in today's stories?

Glossary

Abominable Snowman (*see* **Wild Men**).

Bigfoot (*see* **Wild Men**).

Bunyip A monster that supposedly inhabits Australian lakes and rivers, also called 'Water Devil'.

Cyclopes (singular: cyclops) In Greek mythology, a race of one-eyed giants.

Dragon A reptile-like mythical monster that breathes fire.

Dugong A sea mammal with flippers and a large tail that lives in Asian coastal waters (*see also* **Manatee**).

Evolution The gradual changing of a living thing, from one form into another, over a long period of time.

Extinct An extinct species is one that has died out.

Fossils Remains, such as bones, of long-dead ancient creatures, found moulded in layers of rock.

Frankenstein A character in a book by Mary Shelley who brings to life a monster created from human corpses.

Geep A half-sheep half-goat, created in the 1990s by genetic engineering.

Genes In a living body, the units inherited from the previous generation that pass on certain individual characteristics such as hair or eye colour.

Genetic engineering The alteration of genes in order to change a living thing.

Giant A person who is much taller than normal.

Gigantism The medical condition that causes abnormal growth.

Ice Age A time when the Earth was covered with ice. The last Ice Age ended 10,000 years ago.

Kraken In Norwegian mythology, a gigantic octopus-like sea-monster.

Little people The collective name for beings that are part of Scandinavian, British, Irish and Northern European folklore. They include fairies, elves, dwarves, pixies, trolls, leprechauns and sprites.

Loch Ness Monster The unknown creature that is supposed to inhabit Loch Ness in Scotland.

Lycanthropy A mental illness that causes a person to believe that they have become a wolf.

Manatee A sea mammal that lives in the coastal waters of southern USA.

Mermaid A mythical sea creature that is half-woman, half-fish.

Missing Link The term given to a species of animal between ape and human.

Mutant Something that has altered (mutated) from its normal form.

Myth A traditional story, involving imaginary people and magic, often used to explain mysteries of the natural or human world.

Natural phenomena (singular: phenomenon) Something produced by nature, eg. an earthquake or thunderstorm.

Neanderthal man A type of early human, whose remains were first found in Neanderthal, Germany.

Oar fish A rare species of fish that has a long, flattened, ribbon-like body.

Porphyria A rare disease with symptoms including the baring of teeth, and a need to hide in dark places.

Prehistoric creatures Animals that lived in the time before history was written down.

Rabies A fatal disease suffered by wolves and dogs that can be passed to humans.

Sasquatch (*see* **Wild Men**).

Sea-kangaroo A sea-monster found in Australian mythology.

Sea-serpent A legendary, snake-like sea-monster.

Species A group of living things with shared characteristics, eg. dogs, foxes and wolves belong to the same species.

Sphinx In Greek mythology, a winged creature with a woman's head and a lion's body.

Superstition A widely held but unproven belief.

Vampire In legend, a corpse that comes 'alive' and sucks the blood of the living.

Vampire bat A South American bat that bites and sucks blood.

Werewolf A mythical creature that changes from human form into a wolf.

Wild Men The collective name for the giant, ape-like creatures thought to inhabit the wilds of North America, China and the Himalayas. Also known as Bigfoot, Sasquatch, Abominable Snowman or Yeti.

Wolf children A term for lost or abandoned children found living with wolves.

Yeti (*see* **Wild Men**).

Index

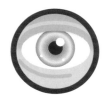